All Time Favorite STANDARDS FOR PIANO

7122049

EDITOR: TONY ESPOSITO

Metro-Goldwyn-Mayer Presents David Lean's Film "DOCTOR ZHIVAGO"

LARA'S THEME FROM "DOCTOR ZHIVAGO"

(Somewhere, My Love)

Music by
MAURICE JARRE

FASCINATING RHYTHM

Music and Lyrics by
GEORGE GERSHWIN
and IRA GERSHWIN

Presto, with abandon

ANYTHING GOES

Words and Music by
COLE PORTER

CANADIAN SUNSET

Music by
EDDIE HEYWOOD

I KNOW THAT YOU KNOW

Music by
VINCENT YOUMANS

BUT NOT FOR ME

Words and Music by
GEORGE GERSHWIN
and IRA GERSHWIN

Play L.H. part legato

From the M-G-M Motion Picture "SWEET BIRD OF YOUTH"

EBB TIDE

Music by
ROBERT MAXWELL

I THOUGHT ABOUT YOU

By JOHNNY MERCER and
JIMMY VAN HEUSEN

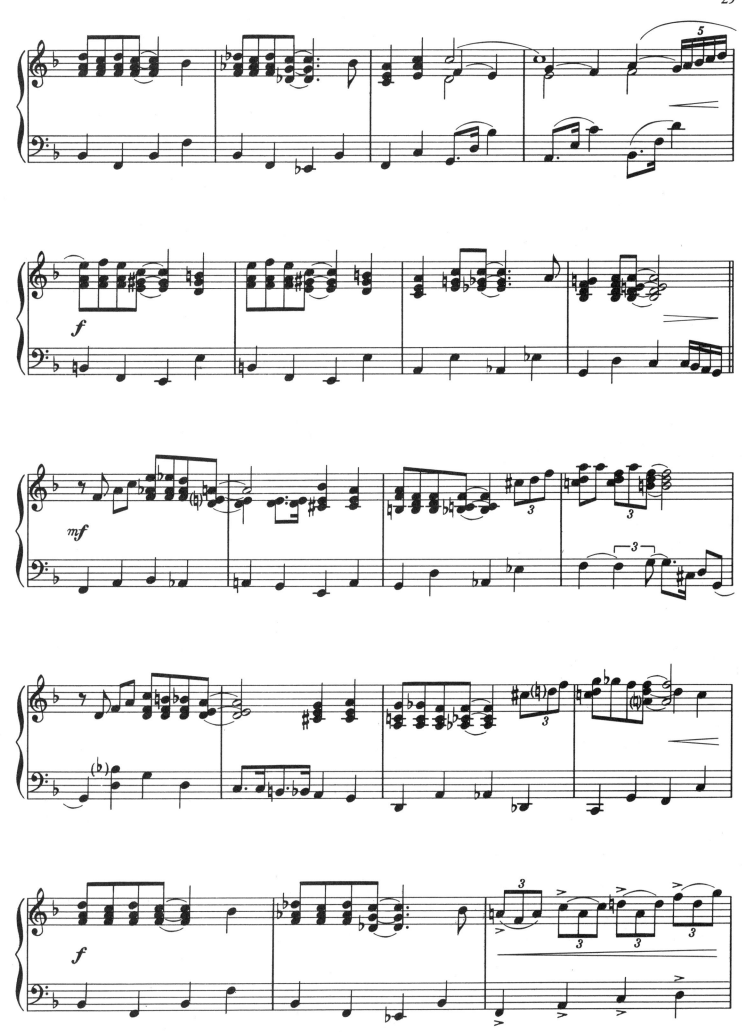

THE GREATEST LOVE OF ALL

Music by
MICHAEL MASSER

EMBRACEABLE YOU

Music and Lyrics by
GEORGE GERSHWIN
and IRA GERSHWIN

LIZA
(All the Clouds'll Roll Away)

Music by
GEORGE GERSHWIN

From the United Artists Motion Picture "ROCKY"

GONNA FLY NOW
(Theme from "Rocky")

By BILL CONTI,
AYN ROBBINS and CAROL CONNORS

I GOT RHYTHM

Music and Lyrics by
GEORGE GERSHWIN
and IRA GERSHWIN

Faster, with abandon

*L.H. is 8va also.

I'M JUST WILD ABOUT HARRY

Words and Music by
NOBLE SISSLE and EUBIE BLAKE

I'VE GOT A CRUSH ON YOU

Music and Lyrics by
GEORGE GERSHWIN
and IRA GERSHWIN

Allegretto giocoso

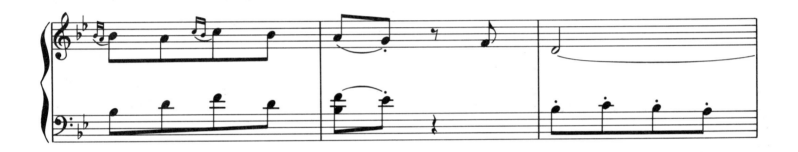

Slowly and sustained

L.H.

R.H.

L.H.
with pedal throughout

rit.

* *The melody (top note of roll) should be played by cross over L.H.*

JUST ONE OF THOSE THINGS

Words and Music by
COLE PORTER

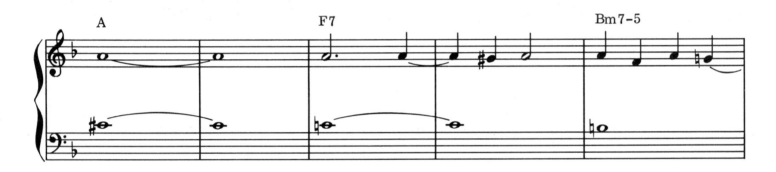

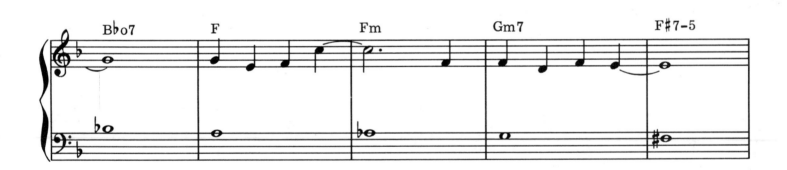

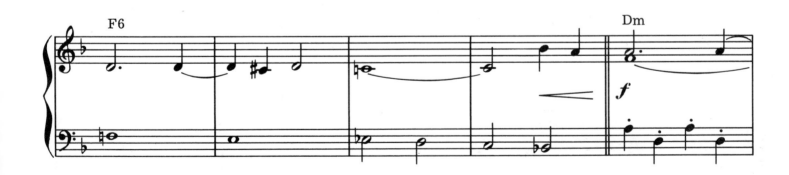

LOW DOWN BLUES

Words and Music by
NOBLE SISSLE and EUBIE BLAKE

D.S. 𝄋 al Coda ⊕

⊕ Coda

NAMELY YOU

By JOHNNY MERCER and
GENE DE PAUL

NIGHT AND DAY

Words and Music by
COLE PORTER

Very broad and free

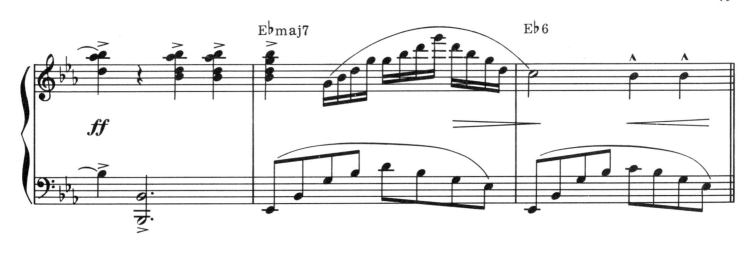

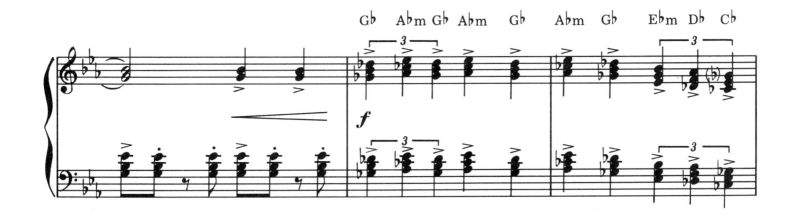

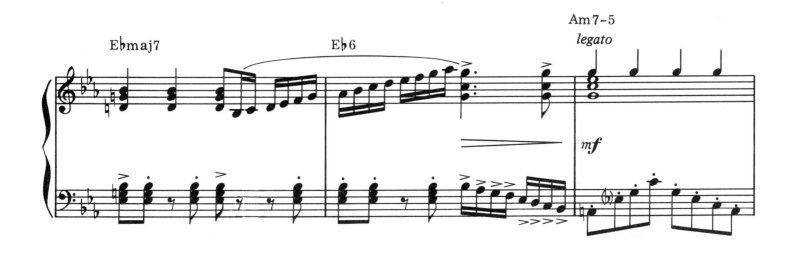

'S WONDERFUL

Music and Lyrics by
GEORGE GERSHWIN
and IRA GERSHWIN

THE SYNCOPATED CLOCK

Music by
LEROY ANDERSON

THEME FROM ICE CASTLES

Music by MARVIN HAMLISCH

KITTEN ON THE KEYS

By
ZEZ CONFREY

SHUFFLE ALONG

Words and Music by
NOBLE SISSLE and EUBIE BLAKE

HERE'S TO MY LADY

By JOHNNY MERCER and
RUBE BLOOM

Slowly, with a steady beat

Slightly Slower
Molto espr.

SOMEONE TO WATCH OVER ME

Music and Lyrics by
GEORGE GERSHWIN
and IRA GERSHWIN

I WANT TO BE HAPPY

Music by
VINCENT YOUMANS

Slowly, but sad
(Bring out)

THE MAN I LOVE

Music and Lyrics by
GEORGE GERSHWIN
and IRA GERSHWIN

Moderately, with a light beat

MORE THAN YOU KNOW

Music by
VINCENT YOUMANS

Slowly, with feeling

From "THE SANDPIPER"

THE SHADOW OF YOUR SMILE

Love Theme from "The Sandpiper"

Arranged by ROGER WILLIAMS

Music by
JOHNNY MANDEL

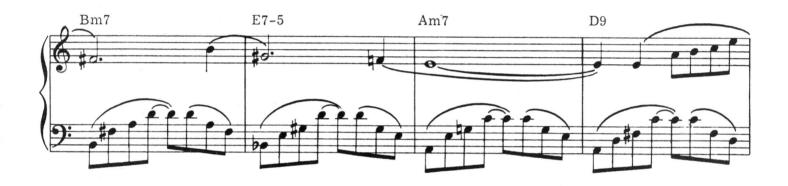

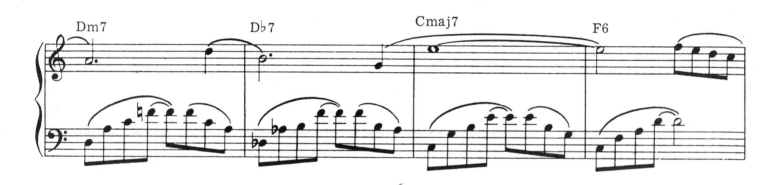

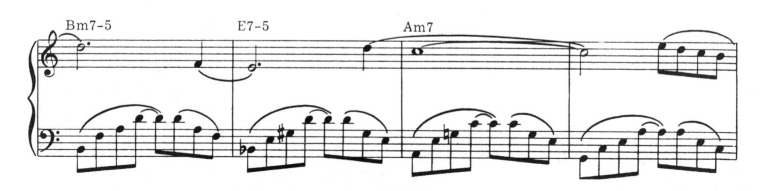

SKYLARK

By JOHNNY MERCER and
HOAGY CARMICHAEL

THEME FROM NEW YORK, NEW YORK

Music by
JOHN KANDER